IMMEL's
New Guide to
BAHRAIN

PETER VINE

IMMEL
Publishing

Phototypeset in Helvetica by
Berry's, Westport, Co. Mayo, Ireland.

Printed and bound in Japan by
Dai Nippon Printing Co., Tokyo.

Design by Jane Stark, Connemara Graphics, Ireland.

ISBN-: 0-907151-48-5

IMMEL PUBLISHING,
Ely House,
37 Dover Street,
London W1X3RB.

Tel. 01 491 1799. Tlx 296582 ELTOUP G. Fax 01 409 1525.

Contents

Grand Mosque at night.

Foreword

In recent years a number of excellent books have been published on various aspects of Bahrain's heritage and modern development. Since the opening of the causeway linking Bahrain to the Arabian mainland we have witnessed a significant increase in the numbers of people making short visits to Bahrain. 'Tourists' is probably the wrong word to describe many of these visitors since most may have a secondary reason for coming here: perhaps to carry out business; maybe as a convenient transit point in their journey; or possibly to visit relatives. One result of this increase is that word of Bahrain's numerous charms has reached a wider audience and more and more people are discovering for themselves the multifaceted appeal of this island nation. For those of us who live here it is easy to become complacent about Bahrain's attractions, taking for granted its abundant sea-foods, exciting sport fishing, ideal sailing and water-sport locations, convenient beaches, wild desert scenery, archaeological and historical sites, abundant wildlife, natural gardens, and special projects such as Al Areen Wildlife Park, or reconstructed and conserved traditional buildings. None of us however fail to appreciate the tremendous strides Bahrain has made in its infrastructural and architectural development in recent years. Modern housing, schools, medical facilities, improved roads and superb hotels, clubs and sports centres have made Bahrain an even more comfortable and attractive place to live.

In line with our modern progress we are increasingly aware of the role history and traditions have played in the evolution of the state of Bahrain. The opening of our new National Museum, a major project by international as well as national standards, is a measure of the importance we place on this aspect of our nationhood.

Peter Vine's first book on Bahrain, *Pearls in Arabian Waters,* was a considerable success. In writing this new guide book he has drawn upon his personal experience of Bahrain and presents an original and fascinating approach to our country. I am confident that within these pages both visitors and residents will find subjects of interest and will be encouraged to discover for themselves the lustrous 'pearls' which the author and photographers have so expertly polished.

Tariq Almoayed,
Minister of Information,
The State of Bahrain.

Introduction

The islands of Bahrain constitute a unique segment of Arabia. Seven thousand years after the land-bridge with the Arabian sub-continent was severed by a gradual rise in sea-level, a new man-made link to the mainland has been created in the form of the Bahrain-Saudi Arabia causeway. This engineering feat enables one to cross in a few minutes a stretch of shallow sea, previously the preserve of graceful wooden dhows driven across the straits by billowing lateen sails and, more recently, by rugged diesel engines. Bahrainis have, since earliest times, maintained a close relationship with the sea, at the same time adapting Bedouin skills in desert survival to their own particular situation.

Evidence from past generations is everywhere apparent in Bahrain, either in the form of a landscape pock-marked with ancient grave-mounds, some over five thousand years old; or in the excavated ruins of intriguing temples like that of Barbar; or in more recent structures such as the Bahrain fort, Arad fort; or indeed many of the existing houses in the older parts of Manama, Muharraq and other towns. Here is a land resplendent with history and culture where links with past traditions remain tenuously intact and where modern progress has been tempered with Bahraini style and a natural empathy towards the country's rich heritage.

This new guide book to Bahrain is not an attempt to explain exactly where to go and what to do in Bahrain. Such a task is already well catered for in regular magazines, up to date newspaper articles and in a number of other publications. The purpose of this book is to enhance awareness of the uniquely attractive qualities of Bahrain, encouraging both visitors and residents to make the most of their time here. It may also prove to be a convenient and attractive gift, summing-up life in Bahrain for relatives and friends who would like to hear more about the country but who have so far not been fortunate enough to visit.

The main part of the book is divided into eight sections each illustrated by a series of pictures high-lighting key aspects of the particular subject.

The Land of Bahrain comprises stony and sandy desert, semi desert, sabkha or salt flats, a distinctive central depression, and naturally irrigated oases where fresh water from underground springs has provided a basis for long-term settlement of the northern part of the main island. The contrast between luscious green date-palm groves and arid brown desert contributes to the immense appeal of Bahrain's landscape. Above all else, Bahrain is a group of islands set in a shallow, yet highly productive sea. The marine environment has played a vital role in the development of Bahrain and Bahrainis continue to retain a natural love of the sea and all things marine. Fishing is both work and play and a love of boats is second nature for Bahrainis.

It has been said that Bahrain is a living and natural museum and there is a great deal of truth in this statement. For the people of Dilmun, inhabiting this area five thousand or so years ago, Bahrain was a paradisal land wherein the god of 'Sweet Waters under the Earth', Enki, was worshipped. Initially Dilmun included parts of the Arabian mainland but, as time passed, the civilisation became centred on Bahrain where the combination of abundant spring water and a strategic maritime

location formed the basis for a flourishing ritual and trading community. Evidence of just how sophisticated the Dilmunites were is provided by the solid geometric construction of their cut-stone temple at Barbar and by the exquisite artifacts recovered from some of the 172,000 or so grave mounds distributed on the island. At its height the ancient city at Qala'at al Bahrain had a population of 7,000 people. By 3800 BP Dilmun, now controlled by the Kassites, had diminished in importance. In subsequent periods under Persian and Greek influence, Bahrain was known as Tylos and famed even then for its fine pearls.

Islam united Bahrainis with the rest of that great religious brotherhood centred in Arabia and focused on Mecca. Bahrain's subsequent history see-sawed between periods of international strife and internal peace. The Portuguese saw in it a great base and, indeed, managed to settle here between 1521 and 1602 when they were supplanted by the Persians. They in turn were eventually ousted, in 1783, by Ahmed Al Khalifa, henceforth known as 'The Conqueror', who thereby established the Al Khalifa dynasty which has continued to this day.

Strongly family orientated, Bahrainis have long been influenced by the traditions of their household, their tribe, their village, their pearling craft, and, of course, their religion. In some cases these traditions live on and survive the pressures of modern-life whereas, in other instances recently exercised traditions are now preserved only by special effort such as government sponsorship of local crafts or through collection and conservation work carried out by the Heritage Centre, the new National Museum, or by other departments under the general direction of the Ministry of Information. For Westerners used to an almost total urban extinction of their own local traditions, the country offers a wonderful glimpse of a uniquely Bahrainised Arabian culture.

The 'Tree of Life', in reality an Acacia tree flourishing almost miraculously in the midst of a generally treeless central depression, is a symbol of the tenacity with which Bahrain's plants and animals cling to life here, squarely facing the challenges of climate and terrain. Both oryx and ostrich once freely roamed this land and can now be seen in their natural habitat at Al Areen Wildlife Park. Sadly the true Arabian ostrich is extinct and it is the African bird which is breeding there, but, in the case of the oryx, Al Areen has played its part in saving this species from extinction. A visit to Al Areen gives one some idea of how the semi-desert once looked before over-grazing by camels and goats denuded much of the natural vegetation. Situated on the migratory paths of many birds moving between northern Asia or Europe and Africa or southern Arabia, Bahrain is a good place for ornithologists, as Mike Hill expertly demonstrates with his bird photographs.

One does not, however, need to be an archaeological or wildlife buff to enjoy Bahrain (although an investigative interest in these subjects will enhance one's pleasure). Bahrain is a place where people work and play hard. Sports are encouraged at all levels and sporting facilities, already excellent, are continually being improved. Souvenir and bargain hunters are seldom disappointed and Bahrain is renowned for its sophisticated Gold Souk and natural pearl shops. Here there can be no doubt that the highest quality jewellery is available, created by skilled artisans. Culinary experts will find a visit to the Spice Souk rewarding while a similar degree of traditionality may be found in perfume shops or in the cloth market.

Innovative building projects have radically transformed the face of modern Bahrain. The Diplomatic area has made a magical transition from a building site to a conglomeration of imaginatively designed buildings. Manama's main corniche is graced by a magnificent Grand Mosque and a superb new National Museum. The new causeway linking Bahrain to Saudi Arabia is one more mega-project contributing towards Bahrain's impressive development. Bahrain's oil and gas finds have helped to fund much of the island's development while these energy industries have spawned a number of other large projects among which the aluminium smelter is one of the most impressive.

Between the pages of this small guide-book all of the above elements, together with others not mentioned, are illustrated. By definition, this is a rather personal view of Bahrain and there are many subjects which have been omitted, either through shortage of space or through the limitations of my own experience. While the book can suggest activities or particular visits there is no substitute for exploring the island one's self, or better still taking a guided tour and perhaps in the process discovering many other aspects of this fascinating country.

The Land

Geologists refer to the structure of Bahrain as that of an eroded dome, a term best understood by studying the geological cross-section below. The terrain on the main island consists of coastal low-lands followed by gently rising slopes terminating in the rim of a crater-like basin known as the 'Central Depression'. In the heart of this depression stands the famous 'Tree of Life', an *Acacia*, demonstrating the species' incredible ability to draw moisture from what appears to be completely dry earth. Camels roam this arid plain, grazing upon stunted plant-life and a prehistoric-looking lizard, the dhab, may also be found here. Devoid of any real mountains, Jebel Dukhan ('Mountain of Smoke'), rising out of the Central Depression, is the highest point on the island, reaching 122m above sea-level. Its marine sedimentary origins are clearly evidenced by conspicuous horizontal strata and a shelly substrate.

The secret of Bahrain's appeal to the ancients, and of its successful and continual colonisation since then, is of course the presence of underground water arriving at the surface in a number of natural springs, the most famous of which is the Adhari pool, Ain Adhari (or the 'Virgin's Pool') – a favourite swimming place where Bahrainis cool-off. Water from such springs is channelled or pumped through irrigation canals to plantations of date-palms or other crops.

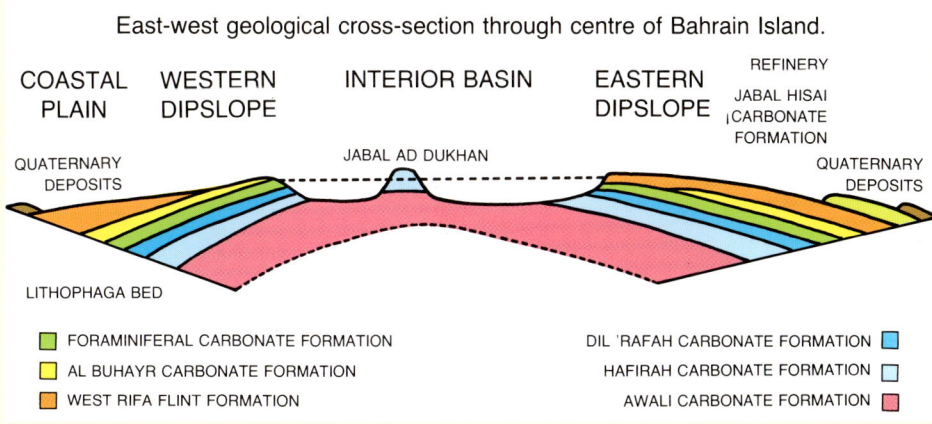

East-west geological cross-section through centre of Bahrain Island.

| COASTAL PLAIN | WESTERN DIPSLOPE | INTERIOR BASIN | EASTERN DIPSLOPE | REFINERY / JABAL HISAI CARBONATE FORMATION |

QUATERNARY DEPOSITS

JABAL AD DUKHAN

QUATERNARY DEPOSITS

LITHOPHAGA BED

🟩 FORAMINIFERAL CARBONATE FORMATION   DIL 'RAFAH CARBONATE FORMATION 🟦

🟨 AL BUHAYR CARBONATE FORMATION   HAFIRAH CARBONATE FORMATION ⬜

🟧 WEST RIFA FLINT FORMATION   AWALI CARBONATE FORMATION 🟥

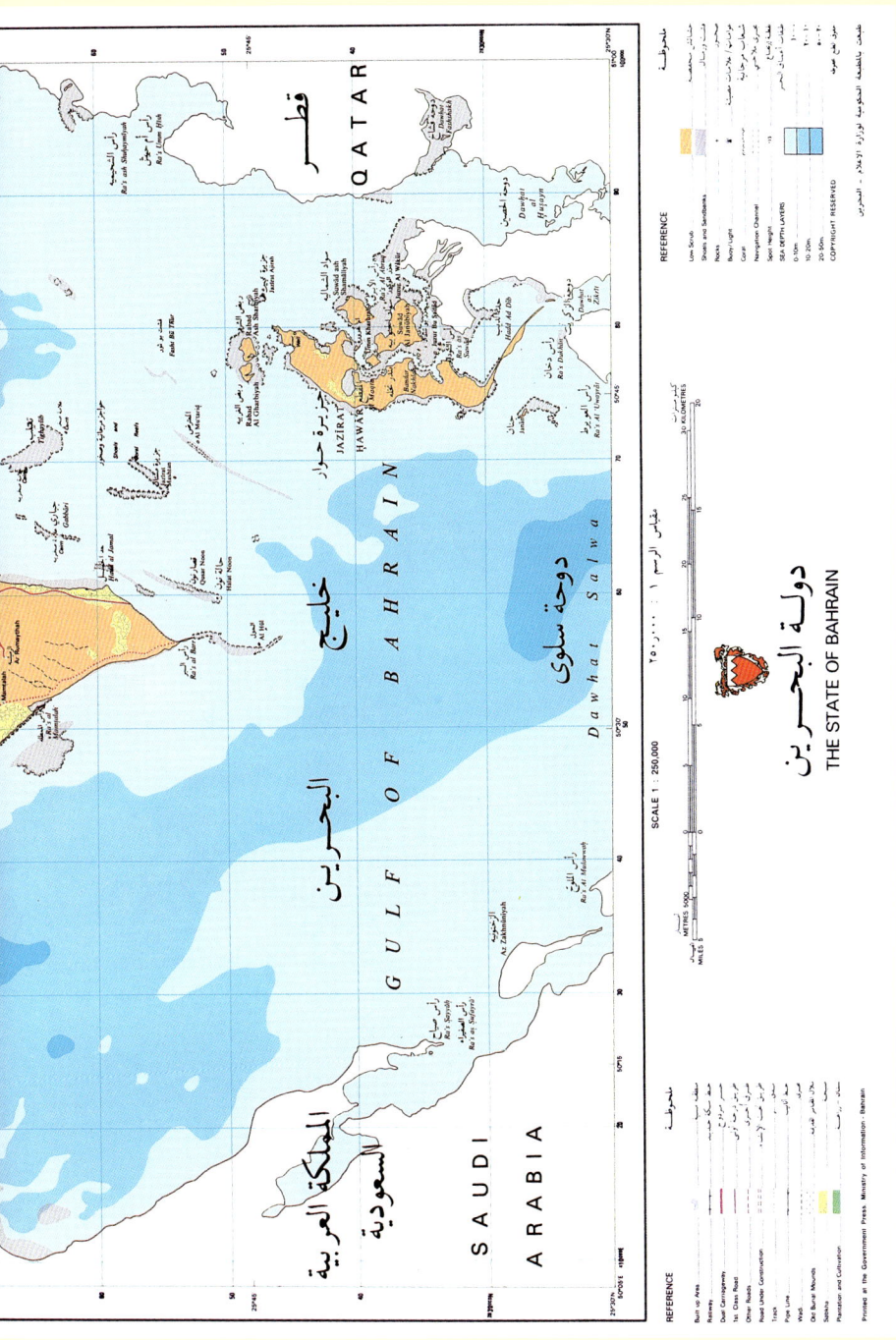

THE STATE OF BAHRAIN

دولة البحرين

SCALE 1 : 250,000

Camels cross the Central Depression, near the 'Tree of Life'.

Palm groves near Qala'at al Bahrain in the north-west of Bahrain.

Opposite: The 'Tree of Life' (Shajarat Al-Hiya) is in fact an old and still flourishing Acacia tree whose roots delve deep into the desert reaching a hidden water-table. The tree stands on a slight hummock which may be caused by the tree itself or perhaps it is a tell, covering the remains of some early settlement. The latter possibility remains to be investigated but signs of Man's early presence here are already available in the form of Stone Age flints recovered from around the 'Tree of Life'.

Ain Adhari (the Virgin's Pool) today forms part of Adhari National Park, a recreation centre. It is one of several large fresh-water springs which traditionally supplied much of Bahrain's sweet-water. The Adhari spring is a popular venue for Bahrainis to cool off, and to practice their diving.

Above: Jebel Dukhan (Mountain of Smoke) is the highest point on Bahrain, reaching 122 metres above sea-level and providing dramatic views of the surrounding countryside. The Tropospheric Scatter Station is a prominent feature on the south-eastern slopes of the 'mountain'.

Right: Agriculture in Bahrain has greatly benefited from improvements in irrigation and growing methods. Apart from dates, a broad range of local vegetables are produced including tomatoes, cabbage, cauliflower, lettuce, carrots, onions, eggplants, beetroot, turnips, potatoes, watermelons, cantaloups, okra, marrow and pumpkin.

Above: Date cultivation in Bahrain is almost as ancient as the advent of Man's presence on the landscape. Bahraini dates have a special reputation for their succulence and sweetness. Early Dilmunites, living here five thousand years ago, relished their dates and suffered (as archaeologists have recently confirmed) the dental consequences.

Overleaf: Date-palm groves provide natural shade and are popular gathering places for young and old alike.

Coast and Sea

Above all else Bahrain is a group of islands set in a shallow, yet highly productive sea. The marine environment has played a vital role in the country's development, both as a natural defensive feature, and as a vital source of food and wealth in the form of pearls. The sea has influenced the thinking of Bahrainis who are outward looking and quick to learn from others.

Bahrain is situated in the Gulf of Salwa, a section of the shallow body of water known as the Arabian Gulf which is connected to the Arabian Sea and the Gulf of Oman through the Straits of Hormuz. Bahraini waters are patterned by coral reefs and shallow banks interwoven by deeper channels through which daily tides flush back and forth, ensuring a high level of mixing, thereby helping to support a rich sea-life.

The principle elements in Bahrain's marine resources are its commercial fish; its abundant shrimps; and its native pearl oysters. The latter are not commercially exploited at present but once provided the mainstay of the nation's economy. Fish and shrimps are caught by both artisinal and commercial fishermen, using a variety of techniques, some of which appear to have originated among Bahraini fishermen. Associated with these rich traditions of pearling and fishing, boat building has long been a local craft and one which has continued, largely in the traditional manner, right up to the present time.

Opposite: Hadra fish-traps form a distinctive feature of Bahrain's sea-scape. The traps straddle inter-tidal and sub-tidal zones and are laid so that fish moving along the shore, as the tide ebbs, are lured by the long wall ('yad' or 'mataam') towards the deeper water and eventually through a narrow slit into the trap ('hawsh' or 'qadil') from which they are later harvested at low-tide.

Opposite: Bahrainis love their fishing, whether as a means of earning a living or as a hobby.

Above: Traditional wooden fishing craft, or Shu'i, powered by diesel engines form the backbone of Bahrain's commercial fishing fleet centred primarily at Sitra.

Right: Commercial fishing boats are all owned by Bahrainis but are frequently crewed today by expatriate fishermen.

Left and below: A deepened enclosure within the 'hawsh' or hadra fish-trap, known as the 'sirr', holds fish alive until they can be harvested at low-tide.

Opposite, above: Artisinal fishing methods have not changed greatly over the years. Traditional semi-spherical small fish-traps, baited with bread, sea-weed or dead fish, are today made from wire instead of woven palm fronds, but they operate in the same manner, catching rabbitfish and other shallow-water species.

Opposite, below: Traditional Hadra fisherman (Vine).

Opposite: Scores of commercial fishing boats tie up at Sitra fishing jetty, prior to their afternoon departure for the prawning grounds or to tend their large gargoor fish-traps.

Left: Produce of both commercial and artisinal catches generally end up at Manama's Fish Market, adjacent to the Vegetable Market.

Below: Bahraini shrimps, primarily Penaeus semisulcatus, are particularly tasty: they are still traded in palm woven baskets at Manama Fish Market.

Porgy (Mylio bifasciatus) *is an abundant fish in local waters (Vine).*

Whitespotted spinefoot or rabbitfish (Siganus canaliculatus) *is caught in wire traps, hadras, with inshore gill nets and as by-catch in shrimp hauls. It is delicious eating and one of the more expensive fish in the market (Vine).*

Shrimp, (Penaeus semisulcatus), *are commercially fished by local craft using medium size trawls. A closed season in spring-time protects spawning females (Vine).*

The best time to visit Manama Fish Market is in the early morning, at around 0530hrs, when the catches are brought to the market, and most trading takes place.

Dried and salted rabbitfish are a delicacy and, before the advent of refrigerators, this method of preservation played an important role in the local economy.

The gold toothless trevally (Gnathodon speciosus) is probably the commonest carangid in Bahraini waters and is caught in gargoor bottom traps and fish trawls.

Left: Wood for Bahrain's boat building industry is mostly imported; planking is constructed from Indian teak whilst the ribs are made from trees known as 'mit' and brought from Iraq, India or Somalia.

Below: Despite their exquisite lines, no plans are laid out before local construction of Arabian dhows. Instead the master builder works from eye, injecting much of his own personality into the finished craft.

Opposite: Ali Jassim Ali has been working for forty years building boats in Bahrain. He began at the age of ten, learning the trade from his father. At the time of writing Ali had three dhows under construction using traditional methods which have hardly changed during the past century or so, despite the widespread encroachment of modern technology.

Sunset near Hidd on Muharraq island.

Ancient Bahrain

The earliest written account of a sea journey, inscribed in the world's oldest epic poem, describes a visit by Gilgamesh to 'Dilmun'. The legend eulogises the ethereal qualities of this distant land where Man is reported to have discovered the secret of immortality. For centuries the identification of Dilmun on modern geographic maps remained a mystery. Gradually however, scholarly translation of early Mesopotamian tablets, combined with detailed archaeological investigations on Bahrain itself, led to the conclusion that Dilmun was centred upon Bahrain and that five thousand years ago a sophisticated and substantial community existed here.

The evidence of this ancient civilisation is abundant and impressive, including the magnificent cut and fitted stone-block walls of the Barbar temple with its sacred well and central place of sacrifice; the hundred and seventy-two thousand or so grave mounds scattered across the main island, and the numerous artifacts and other information gleaned from excavations of these and additional structures.

Dilmun was much more than a romantic vision of the early poets; "... with abundant fresh-water, lying some two days' sail with a following wind from Mesopotamia", it is clear that the Dilmunites were trading partners of their cousins living on the banks of the Euphrates. Bahrain, since these early times, has indeed been part of a much larger canvas, making a significant contribution to civilisation both regionally and globally.

Opposite: Sacred well at Barbar temple built over a natural spring: the remarkable ruins of this ancient temple date from the third millenia BC and is closely linked with Sumerian counterparts from the same era. The sacred well is however a unique feature and is presumably associated with Dilmunite worship of Enki, the God of Spring Waters.

Right: The walls of this Barbar temple, unlike their brick built Sumerian counterparts, are of cut stone blocks; the precision of their construction underlining the considerable sophistication achieved by the Dilmunite civilisation.

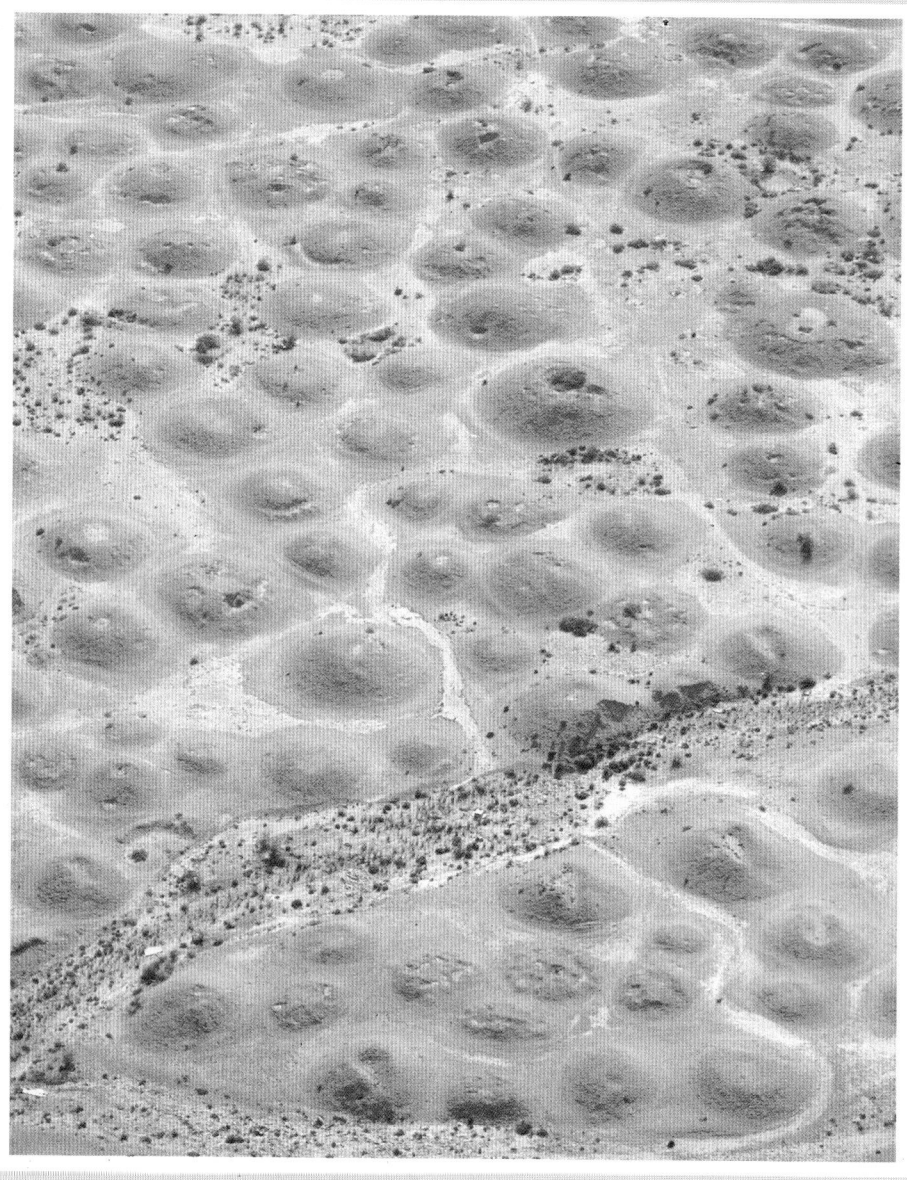

Above: Most recent estimates suggest that at least 172,000 burial mounds are located on Bahrain. Of these, 150,000 are from the Early Bronze Age, (ie, 2800 BC to 1800 BC). The mounds at Sa'ar number around 15,000 and are extremely densely arranged.

Opposite, above: Excavation of grave mounds at Hamad Town has unearthed considerable information about the lives of Dilmunites whose civilisation flourished in Bahrain five thousand years ago (Vine).

Opposite, below: A jar with distinctive zig-zag pattern recovered from a grave near Hamad Town dates from early Dilmun (2500 to 2300 BC).

Above and previous page: Steatite Dilmun seals recovered from archaeological digs on Bahrain are indicators of the degree of trading activity which occurred here four thousand or so years ago. Despite their antiquity (post-Akkadian period, after 2350 BC) seals conserved at Bahrain's National Museum still make very clear imprints of their ancient insignia,as this plasticine impression aptly demonstrates.

Above: A painted goblet recovered from a grave near Aali dates from 2200 to 1600 BC.

Opposite: Alabaster jar recovered from Barbar Temple III dates to around 1800 BC.

Above: Steatite pot from a grave at Sa'ar, dating from 2200 to 1600 BC.

Opposite: Drinking cup from late Dilmun, found at Al Migshaa is attributed to the period 1000 to 330 BC.

Above: A group of glass bottles found
together in one chamber at Sa'ar related to
the Tylos period in Bahrains's history, when
Greek influence permeated the local
civilisation. Two of the three vessels
despatched on an exploratory mission by
Alexander the Great terminated their
voyage through the Gulf in Tylos, identified
as Bahrain.

Opposite: A beautiful example of an
Hellenistic flask recovered from a grave at
Sa'ar, dates from 300 BC to 200 AD.

Above and opposite: Qala'at Arad (Arad Fort) is an Arab defence structure possibly built during the latter half of the sixteenth century. The fort was laid to seige by the Portuguese and a record of this event is preserved in an illustration at the national library in Paris. The fort has recently been painstakingly renovated, using original construction techniques. In profile, the reconstructed towers are distinctly aquiline in appearance.

Old Bahrain

Bahrain, despite its relatively small size and the fact that it is a generally arid group of islands, has experienced an unbroken period of occupation for more than seven thousand years. While evidence of ancient civilisations pattern the landscape in the form of thousands of grave mounds and various excavated buildings, evidence of the influences affecting Bahrain's more recent past are even more tangible, comprising many houses, still standing and in use today. Other old houses have been lovingly preserved so that present and future generations may be provided with a window through which to peer at a rapidly receding past. Large communal structures such as Arad Fort and Qala'at al Bahrain are land-marks of a modern nation and reminders of the country's early struggle for independence from foreign influences.

Perhaps Bahrain's most important historic monument is Masjid Al-Khamis (Al-Khamis Mosque), more than 800 years old, and a fitting reminder of the early influence of Islam in Bahrain's development.

Bahrain's current historic era commenced in 1783 when the Persians were finally ousted from Bahrain and the Al Khalifa dynasty was established there. For the next hundred and fifty or so years Bahrain continued to depend upon pearls and sea-trading for its income, the wealthiest businessmen being successful pearl merchants. Evidence of their life-style, in harmony with both the climate and natural environment, is provided by such beautifully designed houses as Bait Shaikh Isa and Bait Siyadi in the old quarter of Muharraq. The Department of Antiquities has made an excellent job of restoring these buildings as it has also of Bait al Jasra, birthplace of Shaikh Isa bin Salman Al-Khalifa, the present Emir of Bahrain.

Guided visits to old and restored houses help to provide an impression of Bahrain's past, but there is no substitute for making one's own explorations among the narrow streets and old buildings of Muharraq, Manama or other towns on Bahrain. It is hoped that these pages will whet readers' appetites to do just that!

Opposite: Qala'at al-Bahrain, the Bahrain Fort, much more than an impressive defensive structure is located on a very large tell covering a series of seven major occupation levels commencing around 2800 BC; the most recent of these, known to archaeologists as City VII, is the Bahrain Fort which sits on top of the rubble and remains of earlier settlements (Lower: Vine).

Left and below: Masjid Al-Khamis, the Al-Khamis Mosque, is the oldest mosque in Bahrain, probably dating from the second half of the eleventh century or even earlier than this, although it was twice reconstructed, firstly in 1340 AD and secondly in the 15th century when the twin minarets were added (Lower: Vine).

*On these two pages and overleaf:
Siyadi House, situated in the old
quarter of Muharraq, is a fine
example of a 19th century pearl
merchant's house. Here visitors may
admire the high ceilinged majlis with
its vividly stained glass upper
windows, ornately patterned wall-
panels and decorative ceiling.
Design features play more than an
aesthetic function however, with
natural cooling and control of light
being prime considerations cleverly
and very pleasingly implemented by
traditional architectural methods.*

Opposite: Interior decorations of a pearl merchant's house, Muharraq (Morris).

Bait al-Jasra is a traditional and beautifully conserved building in the old pearl-diving village of Al Jasra. Built by Shaikh Hamad bin Abdulla Al-Khalifa in 1907, the house was the birthplace of the Emir of Bahrain, Shaikh Isa bin Salman Al-Khalifa. Rooms within the house have been carefully furnished to recapture much of the atmosphere which pertained here at the beginning of the century. When Shaikh Isa was two years old the family moved to West Rifaa and Bait al-Jasra fell into disrepair until its recent restoration in 1986. The house is open to the public.

This page and opposite: Manama and Muharraq have many examples of old houses built in the traditional manner using a mixture of "forrosh" (slabs of gypsum), coral stones, 'yedh'a' (fibres drawn from the trunk of a dead palm tree), gypsum, bamboo, woven palm-matting and palm trunks. Houses were designed to combine aesthetic appeal and traditional style with practical qualities such as natural climatic control, security and social privacy (Vine).

Right: Door detail at the house of Shaikh Isa, Muharraq (Vine).

Overleaf: Beautifully carved wooden doors of Manama's old Law Courts (Vine).

Traditional Bahrain

Despite its current strides in the name of progress, embracing the modern international lifestyle of the twentieth century, modern Bahrain remains inextricably linked to the past, valuing its traditions more and more as the hardships, excitement, comradeship and other shared experiences of the old pearling days recede into distant memory and local folk-lore. Bahrainis, warm, generous, hospitable, relaxed and confident are an essential part of what makes Bahrain a special place; this strength of character apparent in so many of Bahrain's inhabitants is surely based on the conservation of stable traditional values.

Visitors interested to learn about Bahrain's traditions could do no better than to visit its unique Cultural Heritage Centre, at Manama's old Law Courts, and the quite magnificent National Museum. In addition to these displays, there are many traditional aspects of life in Bahrain which are still an integral part of the daily routine including characteristic Bahraini clothing, hospitality, greetings, coffee drinking, 'hubble-bubble' pipe smoking, and various crafts. Among the latter are those associated with pearls and gold jewellery, cloth-weaving, palm-weaving, pottery, tin smiths, coffee-pot makers, blacksmiths and of course traditional sporting skills such as falconry and horsemanship. These pages provide a brief taste of the colour, variety and indeed the magic of traditional Bahrain.

Opposite: Traditional Bahraini marriage bedroom displayed at the Heritage Centre in Manama.

Left and opposite: In their normal daily lives Bahraini women wear the traditional black cloak or abbaya as their outer garment but, on special occasions such as weddings or feasts, much more colourful garments are displayed like this exquisite gold embellished Bahraini bridal dress and jewellery modelled at the Heritage Centre.

Right: Henna is used to decorate hands and feet, especially on celebratory occasions, using patterns which have been passed down from generation to generation. Local folklore maintains that henna strengthens hands and feet and helps to prevent balding: this is a widely held view throughout the Arab world, and modern science may yet confirm that the henna plant does indeed contain biochemicals with such properties.

Above and right: A young Bahraini girl models a traditional Bahraini dress used at formal occasions.

Hassan Al-Arrayed, one of the last remaining traditional Bahraini pearl merchants, grades a small portion of his collection of natural Gulf pearls at his shop in Manama Souk.

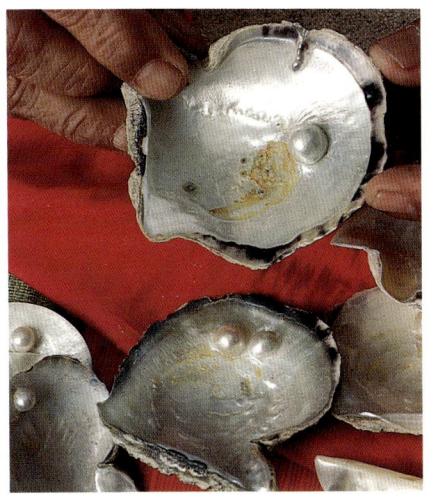 

Above left: Pearl diving mythology recounts that pearls are formed when the pearl mollusc swims to the surface during rain-storms and opens its shell to take in drops of rain-water which later transform into pearls. Scientists, however, insist that pearls arise from the coating of sand grains or other foreign bodies with pearly nacreous layers otherwise used to line the inner surfaces of the shell valves.

Above right: Craftsman piercing minute seed pearl with a hand operated bow-drill.

Below: Bahrain has long been recognised for its production of some of the highest quality natural pearls existing anywhere in the world. Despite the commercial onslaught of cultured pearls, led by the Japanese, there remains a special mystique and appreciation for natural Bahraini pearls which may still be purchased in Manama.

Above: Scale model of pearling boat and crew at the Heritage Centre.

Right: In order to protect their hands from coral cuts and scratches, divers wore leather finger thimbles or 'khabat'.

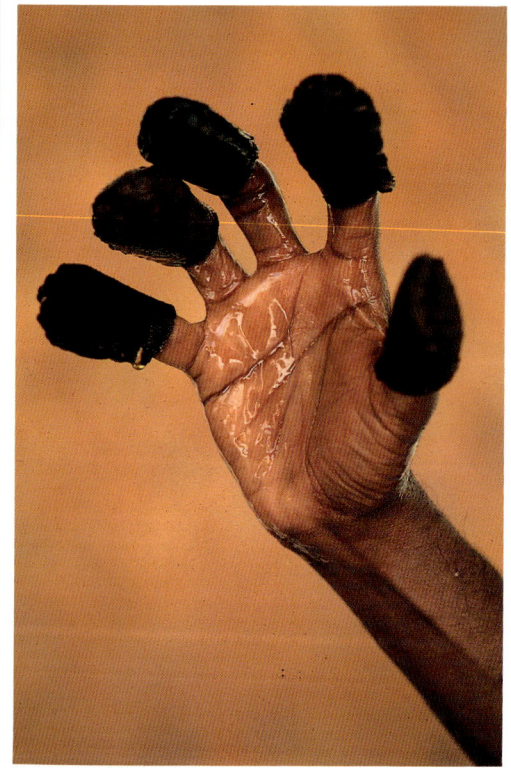

An essential element in the traditional Bahraini welcome is presentation of 'Gahwa' or cardamon-flavoured coffee. Accoutrements of this ritual comprise an elegantly shaped and intricately patterned silver, bronze or copper 'dalla' or coffee jug and small handleless cups or 'fanajeen'.

Sadly, the craft of coffee-pot making is a dying art in Bahrain but we are fortunate that Yasser Yousif El Ansari has taken-up the trade, learnt from a seven year apprenticeship under a recently retired and still famous coffee pot maker, Sayed Ali. Yasser takes about ten days to make a single pot which he sells for around BD90 to BD130 or more each, depending upon the materials used and type of finish.

Different villages in Bahrain are renowned for particular crafts, the art of cloth-weaving being associated with Bani Jamra. In the old days, some of the best sails for dhows were made here and cloth woven for the 'irdeh' (a type of abbaya) was among the finest obtainable anywhere, characteristically decorated with red and gold thread. In earlier times more than a hundred workshops were located in the village, now the Department of Tourism and Antiquities is taking measures to encourage a revival of the ancient craft by marketing Bani Jamra hand woven ties at the tourist shop situated at Bab al Bahrain, and in other centres.

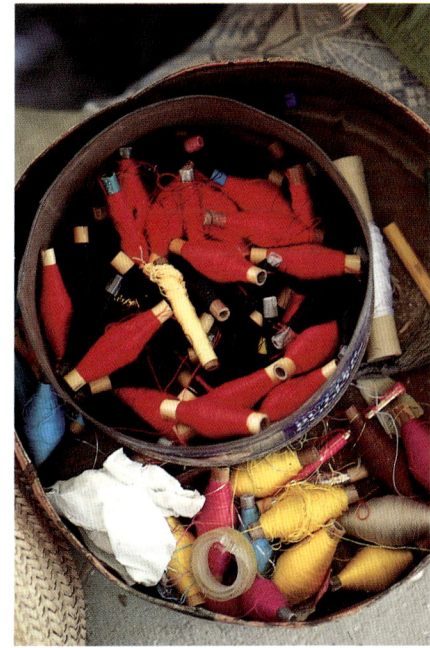

Left: The Heritage Centre has been a focus for study, preservation and display of traditional and cultural aspects of Bahraini life. Housed in the old Law Courts, the Centre contains a variety of displays depicting the country's cultural heritage.

Below: A collection of locally made palm-woven basket-work at the Heritage Centre.

The centre for basket-weaving is the ancient village of Karbabad. Shaded by the same date-palms from which they derive their raw materials, weavers continue to practise their traditional craft (Lower: Vine).

The craft of pottery is usually associated with the village of Aali where the main pottery industry is run by three brothers who produce the container section for hubble-bubble water-pipes or 'gidawa', children's money boxes and a variety of pots and jugs.

Left: A locally made 'gidu' or water-pipe is enjoyed on the edge of Muharraq's southern shore-line.

Below: Traditional hardware stores in old Manama display a variety of locally made goods from potters, tin-smiths, and charcoal burners together with sandalwood, tobacco and other oriental wares (Vine).

Right: Ladles and funnels are among the utensils manufactured by tinsmiths in the souk.

Below: The old wooden pearl-divers' chest provided tin-smiths with inspiration for the metallic equivalent – a popular means of packing personal belongings.

Traditional perfume shops in Bahrain resemble an Aladdin's cave with hundreds of colourful glass bottles containing a wide range of natural substances available for blending into just the right fragrance.

Left: Bahrain's older generation have lived through a period of rapid change and development. Their experiences are unique, spanning the transition from a pearling and fishing maritime economy to the discovery of oil followed by industrial growth and huge improvements in social amenities.

Right: Bahrain's musical tradition is extremely strong, pervading most aspects of life. The oud, shown here, is a favoured instrument for accompanying traditional songs, frequently love lyrics from Nabati poetry.

*Above: The wooden horse depicted here,
and displayed at the Heritage Centre,
represents the traditional parade ceremony
associated with celebrations at the end of
Ramadan.*

While researching this book we asked to see a trained falcon whereupon we were introduced to this magnificent gyr, not one of the local species but a long term resident of the Falcon Centre where it is kept for breeding purposes. Traditional local hunting birds are saker and peregrine falcons while the houbara bustard was the main prey with young gazelle, hare and stone curlew also being taken.

Above: The Arabian thoroughbred horse is truly at home in Bahrain and commands a very special place in the hearts of Bahrainis. Once used as a means of transport and as a mount in battle, the horse is today appreciated for its sheer beauty and fine sporting qualities. Throughout the winter months, weekly race meetings are held at the main race-track west of Awali.

Natural Bahrain

Since earliest times visitors to Bahrain have remarked upon aspects of its natural history, whether referring to the wildlife in and around its fresh-water springs; to the quality and prolificity of its dates; to abundant shrimps and fish; or to its high quality pearls. As we have seen already at the beginning of this book Bahrain is a land of contrasting environments and its natural history is greatly influenced by this fact. On the one hand, true desert species live here while, on the other, some forms are completely tied to fresh-water habitats. Demarcation lines between arid desert and fertile plantations are often abrupt, forming natural barriers controlling distribution of many local species. Whereas Man's impact on the natural environment has often operated against the survival interests of plants and animals, this is not entirely the case in Bahrain since desalination has increased the quantities of surface water in some areas leading, in turn, to more birds and other creatures settling here.

Bahrain's natural history has been reviewed in several recent books including: *An Introduction to the Wildlife of Bahrain* by Dr. Mike Hill and Paul Webb; *Wildflowering Plants of Bahrain* by Christopher and Marion Cornes (Immel); and *Pearls in Arabian Waters,* also published by Immel, in which the present author gives a summary of current knowledge regarding Bahrain's natural environment.

Visitors to Bahrain are strongly advised to take time to appreciate the islands' fascinating natural history. A good place to begin exploring Bahrain's wild heritage is at the 'Tree of Life', standing solitary and erect in the heart of the Central Depression. The prehistoric dhab may be seen here sunning itself out in the open during the middle of the day, whilst, towards sunset, the area takes on an especially appealing aspect as the reddening sky appears to set this unique acacia's foliage alight. Elsewhere, one may explore among sandy desert or wander through fertile, cultivated areas where a variety of birds add both music and colour to the surroundings. Seas around Bahrain literally abound with life as a visit to the local fish-market attests. Whilst water clarity is often affected by suspended sand or silt, snorkel and SCUBA diving are nevertheless popular and rewarding pastimes.

We are indebted to Dr. Mike Hill for contributing some of his excellent wildlife pictures to this brief presentation of Bahrain's natural history.

*Left and overleaf:
'Tree of Life'.*

Centre: Arabian oryx at Al Areen are offspring of the breeding nucleus established in 1964 as part of 'Operation Oryx'. Successful captive breeding of oryx in Bahrain and other countries has raised the possibility of their re-introduction into the wild (Vine).

Below: The Arabian ostrich is unfortunately extinct but this African species, Struthio camelus *has been introduced to Bahrain where it is breeding at Al Areen Wildlife Centre.*

This page: The dhab or spiny-tailed lizard, Uromastyx microlepis, is a prehistoric looking creature which was once very common on Bahrain. A favourite meat of the Bedouin, Dhab have suffered from hunting pressures throughout their range, but at Al Areen a conservation programme has led to a considerable build-up in population and visitors are quite likely to experience close-encounters with these endearing reptiles (Left and below: Vine).

Above: The rat snake (Coluber ventromaculatus) *is non-venomous and sometimes seen in Bahrain's cultivated areas such as date-palm groves or gardens (Hill).*

Below: Marsh frog (Rana ridibunda) *is the only species of frog occurring on Bahrain where it is quite common in drainage ditches and ponds (Hill).*

The lime swallow-tail butterfly (Papilio demoleus) *is the largest and most conspicuous of Bahrain's butterflies (Hill).*

Above: The long-eared desert hedgehog is a nocturnal insectivore living in both desert and cultivated areas on Bahrain (Hill).

Below: The lesser jerboa, Jaculus jaculus, *is readily identifiable by its three-toed hind-foot and the prominent black and white markings at the end of the tail (not shown here (Hill).*

The crested lark, Galerida cristata, *a widespread lark throughout the Middle-East, is a frequent source of bird-song in open-country (Hill).*

The Kentish plover, Charadrius alexandrinus, *a common shore-bird, is frequently observed on sand-flats, near low-water. A resident breeder, it's nest consists of a shallow unlined scrape on dry ground (Hill).*

The rufous bushchat, Cercotrichas galactotes, *a summer visitor, locally breeding species on Bahrain, nests among date-palm groves (Hill).*

The white-eared bulbul, Pycnonotus xanthopygos, *a common resident breeding species, usually nests in gardens or date-palm groves (Hill).*

Above: The ring-necked parakeet or rose-ringed parakeet, Psittacula krameri, *is a resident breeding species in Bahrain where it may sometimes be seen in small flocks of up to forty or so birds. It is likely that this species has become established in Bahrain from escaped cage-birds (Hill).*

Right and opposite: Wild sheep, Ovis ammon, *still live in the wild among Oman's high mountains. At Al Areen the species is being successfully bred in captivity, the lambs, shown here with their keeper, possessing a distinctly gazelle like appearance.*

Above: The date-palm tree, Phoenix dactylifera, *is known locally as 'Nakhale', and has been successfully cultivated on the island for several thousand years since its presumed introduction to Bahrain from neighbouring regions. The local climate appears to be particularly suitable for growing dates, a vital constituent in the diet of Bahrainis since the earliest recorded civilisation. Indeed, Dilmun was renowned for the quality of its sweet dates which were frequently used as sacred offerings.*

Opposite above: Bahrain's natural pearl-beds are still flourishing and producing high quality pearls. Recruitment to the population remains strong and on many beaches vast quantities of young shells accumulate (Vine).

Opposite below: Bahrain's shallow-water coral reefs are characterised by species resistant to sediment, and by sea-weeds which are fed upon by an array of molluscs and echinoderms, including the black-spined Echinothrix *seen here (Vousden).*

Swimming pool at Hotel Diplomat.

Recreational Bahrain

Bahrain offers numerous opportunities for relaxation, sport and entertainment providing essential relief from a competitive and challenging work environment. Bahrainis themselves are keen sportsmen with an interest in traditional pursuits such as horse racing, as well as a healthy enthusiasm for team-sports like football. In recent years there has been an upsurge in athletics and in all keep-fit activities. Training and playing facilities are well provided for with, for example, an impressive football and sports stadium as well as modern horse race tracks. A number of private members clubs provide for special interest groups such as power boat racing, yacht racing, windsurfing, water-skiing, golf, tennis and other sports.

The new causeway has provided a considerable stimulus to tourism in Bahrain with increasing numbers of people staying for short holidays. Luxurious hotels provide all the service and leisure facilities which the discerning international traveller has come to expect: swimming pools and indoor health centres fitted with jacuzzi, sauna, and training equipment are standard features while many also have tennis courts.

Gold or pearl jewellery is usually high on visitors' shopping lists. Manama's Gold Souk provides a powerful lure since one can still shop among the more atmospheric, old-style gold shops or enter the modern Gold Souk to discover a similar range of jewellery on equally resplendent display but benefiting (in summer at least) from the luxury of an air-conditioned environment. Gift and souvenir shopping in Bahrain need not however be restricted to jewellery for a walk into the older parts of the souk brings one in close contact with Arabian traditions and culture. The Spice Souk, redolent with the aroma of the East, is full of exotic herbs and spices in their raw form, often displayed in sacks or on large trays while spectroscopical arrays of vividly coloured materials spill over the shop fronts in the Cloth Souk.

A special interest in archaeology is not a prerequisite for an enjoyable visit to Bahrain's excellent historic displays at the National Museum, to the Heritage Centre and the preserved houses or archaeological remains which abound throughout the country. One of the best aspects of living in, or just visiting, Bahrain is the wide range of opportunities it presents for one to enjoy life in these peaceful and enchanting islands.

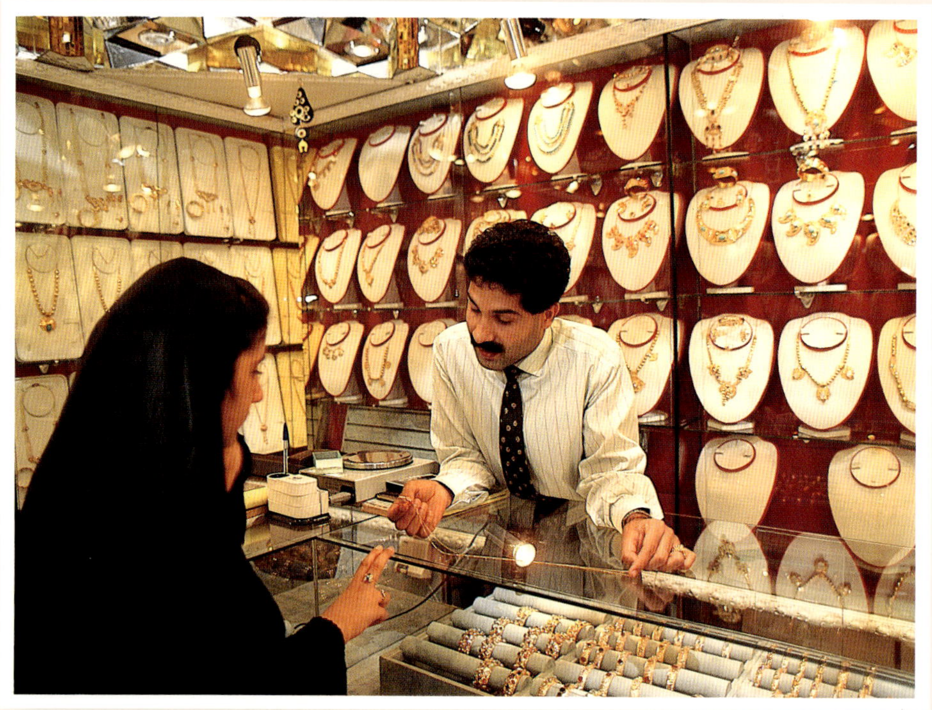

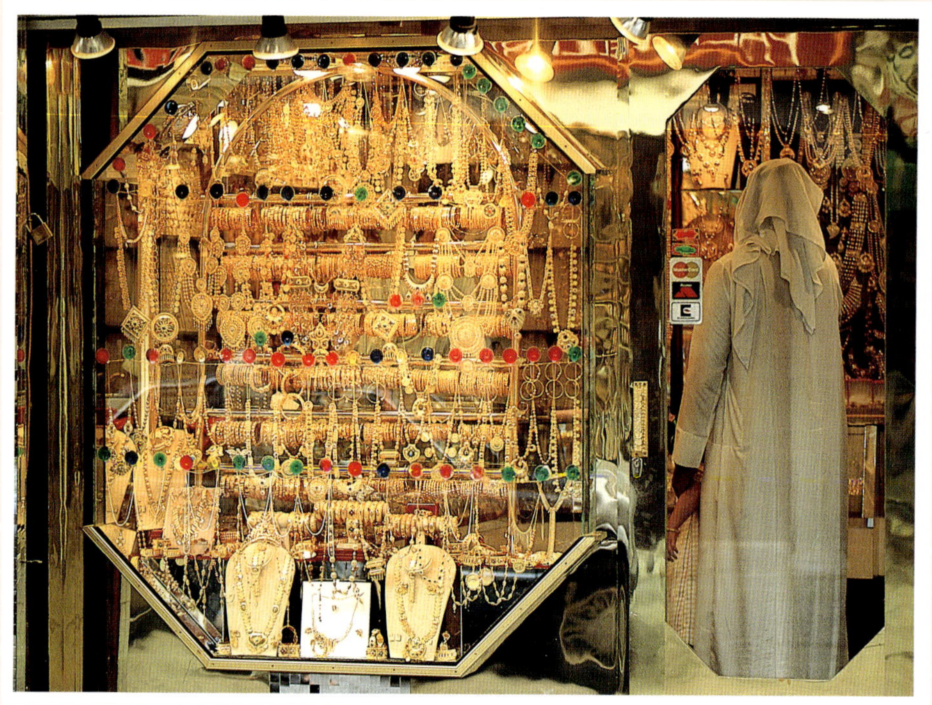

Sheraton Shopping Complex.

Street scene in old Manama's Textile Souk.

Bahrain's taxi drivers are friendly and welcoming to visitors.

Cloth-seller and materials in Manama.

Grading and weighing natural pearls.

Bab Al Bahrain.

In the Spice Souk.

Manama Textile Souk.

New National Museum with Marina Club swimming pool in foreground.

Pearling once formed the mainstay of Bahrain's economy, pearls from Bahrain becoming famous all over the world. Whilst Japanese pearl culture effectively precipitated a collapse to the once flourishing fishery, natural pearls are still sold in Bahrain where the traditions of pearling retain a treasured position at the cultural heart of the nation.

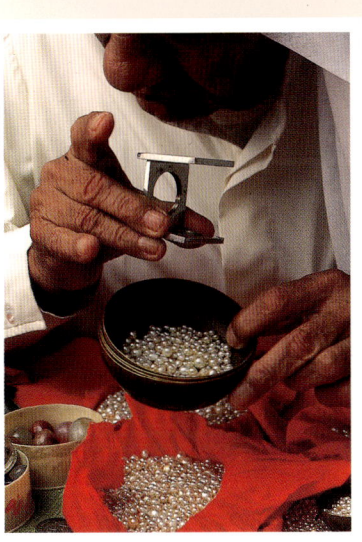

Above: The Marina Club is a favourite base for many of Bahrain's power boat owners.

Below: Bahrain Yacht Club has a strong racing tradition and a particularly enthusiastic group of hobbycat sailors. It's marina provides a safe anchorage for many sailing yachts and power craft.

On June 1st, 1932, oil began to flow from Bahrain's first oil-well at a rate of 9,600 barrels per day making Bahrain the first oil producer in the region and heralding a new era for the country.

On 11th April, 1986, the last link in the causeway joining Bahrain and Saudi Arabia was closed when His Highness Shaikh Khalifa Bin Sulman Al-Khalifa pressed a button causing the final section of bridgework to drop into place. The causeway has already increased the number of visitors to Bahrain and is confidently expected to have a positive economic impact.

New Bahrain

Bahrain's newest era might be said to have commenced in 1971 when the country became a sovereign state under its ruler Shaikh Isa bin Salman Al-Khalifa. Furthering their efforts to strengthen political stability, Bahrain became a member of the Gulf Cooperation Council in 1981 and has remained actively involved in regional issues, supporting moves to achieve overall development throughout the Gulf.

Much of Bahrain's development has been funded by exploitation of its oil and gas reserves. The Bahrain Petroleum Company was originally a wholly owned subsidiary of the Standard Oil Company of California but the Government took a sixty percent stake in BAPCO in 1975. Today the oil industry is managed by Bahrain National Oil Company, BANOCO, which is a fully integrated company responsible for all aspects of oil and gas exploitation from exploration and drilling to distribution and marketing both locally and internationally. Refining is still carried out at BAPCO's Sitra refinery. Apart from oil, Bahrain has important reserves of natural gas, enough, it has been estimated, to last for the next fifty years.

Bahrain's agriculture, representing only two percent of GDP, hardly creates a bleep on the over-all economic picture of the islands. Several plans being currently implemented should greatly increase local food production and raise the level of self-sufficiency in food.

Bahrain's oldest industrial giant is the Bahrain Aluminium Company, ALBA, which commenced its operations in the same year as sovereign independence, 1971. During 1987, 180,344 tonnes of metal was produced, more than 10,000 tons above the plant's rated capacity! Much of this raw metal was processed locally with 20,369 tonnes of liquid metal going to Bahrain Atomisers and Midal; 6,184 tonnes of extrusion billet to BALEXCO, and 37,984 tonnes of rolling ingot to the Gulf Aluminium Rolling Mill Company (GARMCO). The latter now requires 70,000 tonnes of rolling ingots annually! Success of these Aluminium based companies have encouraged a number of other industrial ventures to base themselves in Bahrain helping to create one of the most diversified concentrations of heavy industrial projects in the Gulf.

The recession of the 80's did not miss Bahrain and, like every other country in the region, budget estimates have received careful attention. Nevertheless Bahrain retains all the best features of an entrepot centre with a vibrant commercial sector and a vigorous financial services division. Many companies are situated in down-town Manama or its adjacent Diplomatic area where architects have vied with each other to create eye-pleasing modern buildings especially adapted to the local scene. It is this blend of old and new which helps to make Bahrain so interesting and such an enjoyable place to visit or live.

Oil well number 239, like many of Bahrain's pumping stations, has been decorated, in this case as a hoopoe.

BAPCO's Sitra refinery is one of the oldest refineries in the Gulf but constant upgrading and modernisation have kept it in business.

BAPCO takes a keen interest in their own employees, helping to create a happy workforce.

Painting a new oil storage tank at BAPCO's Sitra Tank Farm.

*Above: Inside the vault room of Bahrain
Monetary Agency millions of dinars are
counted daily.*

Alumina is separated by electrolysis into aluminium metal and oxygen in a bath of molten cryolite (melt) at about 965 degrees Centigrade. This takes place in carbon-lined pots above which are suspended huge electric poles, the anodes, while the carbon lining of the pots act as cathodes to which are drawn positively charged aluminium ions: these lose their charge to the cathode and thus become aluminium. On entering ALBA's Pot Room one is requested to remove all electrical appliances such as digital watches since the electrical field is so great that these are considerably affected, often stopping or running in reverse!

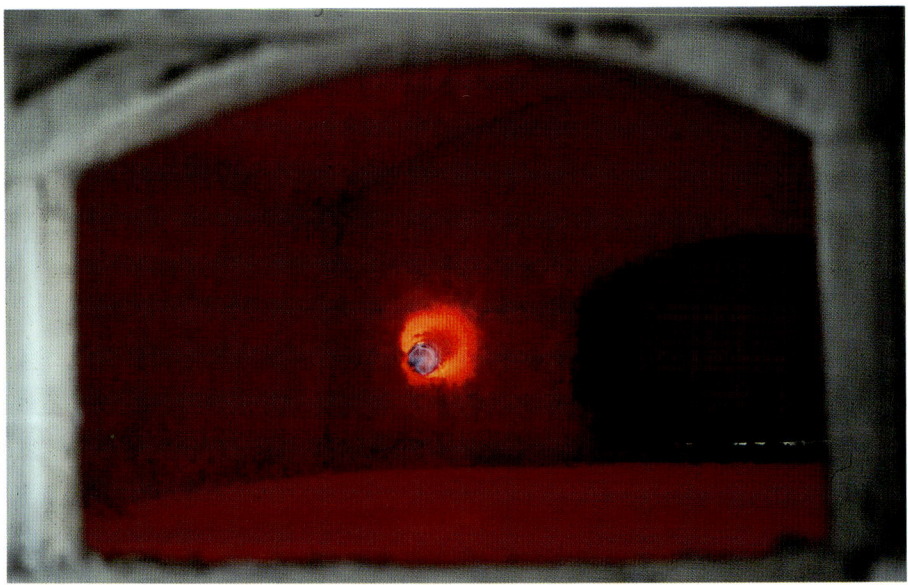

The Arab Shipbuilding and Repair Yard, ASRY, was established by OAPEC in 1977. It specialises in repairs and maintenance of large ships such as oil tankers which frequent Gulf shipping routes.

Opposite: Early morning in Manama.

Opposite: Reflected view of the minaret at Masjid Al-Faadhil mosque.

Above: Bahrain's new Grand Mosque is situated on Manama corniche.

Left: Bait Al-Koran (House of the Korans) has been constructed to house a unique collection of Holy Korans and other manuscripts with the purpose of promoting intellectual and religious ideals. The building incorporates a mosque, library, auditorium, Koran School and a museum with five exhibition halls.

Left: Motif above entrance to new Law Courts in Manama.

Below: Modern building in Diplomatic area.

The New National Museum at night.

The Causeway.

A Fifty Dinar gold coin depicting the head of H H The Amir, Shaikh Isa bin Salman Al-Khalifa.

Acknowledgements

This book would not have been written were it not for the encouragement I received from the Bahrain Ministry of Information. I take special pleasure in thanking His Excellency the Minister of Information, Tariq Almoayed for the practical assistance I received while working on this interesting project. I must also express my deep appreciation to Ahmed Al Sherooqi, Director of Public Relations and Media with whom this publication was originally conceived, following discussions upon available information sources about Bahrain, and from whom I received many useful ideas and valuable guidance.

For presentation of Bahrain's rich archaeological and folkloric heritage I relied heavily upon national resource centres in the form of Bahrain Heritage Centre and the new National Museum, both under the directorship of Shaikha Nayala Ali Khalifa to whom I offer my thanks for her willing cooperation despite the pressing demands of a challenging schedule prior to opening of the National Museum.

Many organisations and companies welcomed us into their establishments to gather material for the book. Unfortunately space prevents thanking them all individually so pictures and captions must speak for themselves. To all those who had a hand in assisting us in our work I should like to say "thank you".

The vast majority of pictures in this book were taken by Adam Woolfitt who accompanied me on one intense visit to Bahrain. He arrived wondering what there would be to photograph but on departure admitted that he would need at least six months work to do justice to what he has seen during his all too brief stay. Wildlife pictures were mostly taken by Dr. Mike Hill who is well known for his excellent book on Bahrain's natural history as well as many other photographic contributions to our knowledge of bird-life, both in Bahrain and further afield.

Further impetus for producing a picture guide to Bahrain came from Leif Munksgaard, Manager of Family Bookshops and Mohammed Hanif, Manager of Al Hilal Bookshops. I am grateful to them for their sincere advice and encouragement.

Index